© Copyright 2024 - All rights reserved

The content contained within this book may not be reproduced, duplicated or transmitted without direct written permission from the author or the publisher.

Under no circumstances will any blame or legal responsibility be held against the publisher, or author, for any damages, reparation, or monetary loss due to the information contained within this brief; either directly or indirectly.

Legal Notice:

This book is copyright protected. This book is only for personal use. You cannot amend, distribute, sell, use, quote or paraphrase any part, or the content within this book, without the consent of the author or publisher.

Disclaimer Notice:

Please note the information contained within this document is for educational and entertainment purposes only. All effort has been executed to present accurate, up to date, and reliable, complete information. No warranties of any kind are declared or implied. Readers acknowledge that the author is not engaging in the rendering of legal, financial, medical or professional advice.

The Modern Guide to Paid Advertising for Business Owners

A Quick-Start Introduction to Google, Facebook, Instagram, YouTube, and TikTok Ads

Preface

Hello, reader!

I would like to first note that this book is intended as a quick, easy guide to modern advertising platforms that will introduce you to the modern advertising landscape and give you the tools you need to go out into the world and use these tools, starting immediately after you finish the text.

It is not an end-all guide, nor exhaustive in its analysis. If that is what you are looking for, I suggest you go elsewhere. If you *are* looking for the absolute essentials, tips, and tricks to get you up to speed on the topic, welcome to *The Modern Guide to Paid Advertising for Business Owners*.

Introduction

People and companies skilled at paid advertising essentially have access to a money printer. There is an excess of advertising channels available, ranging from Facebook and TikTok to Google and YouTube. Most ads are intended to sell a product or service, though some large companies run massive campaigns just to build brand goodwill. Good ads designed to sell a product or service are lifetime profitable; the profit accrued from the ads is greater than the ad spend not necessarily in the short-term but considering derived lifetime customer value (LTV).

Since paid advertising is so scalable and reaches so many hundreds of millions of people, breakeven or profitable adverts are an incredibly valuable tool. Of course, online advertising isn't a secret, and it isn't easy. Many ad operators operate at a loss to drive traffic and sales to their products in the hope that the paid marketing eventually builds organic momentum.

No matter the objective profitability of ad spend, a person with the ability to improve the effectiveness of a company's ads, no matter what that effectiveness is, is worth big dollars to that organization. A person who excels at paid advertising can drive enormous amounts of targeted traffic to websites of their choosing, and many individual entrepreneurs utilize this in their own pursuits.

So, what does paid advertising entail? Generally, advertising involves a funnel. Each advertising funnel has several stages, which introduce people to the brand and business at the top-most level, and turns them into paying customers at the bottom-most level. Funnels don't always need to funnel toward a purchase point, just toward the KPIs identified in the brand and social strategy sections. For example, consider the following funnel of a theoretical business:

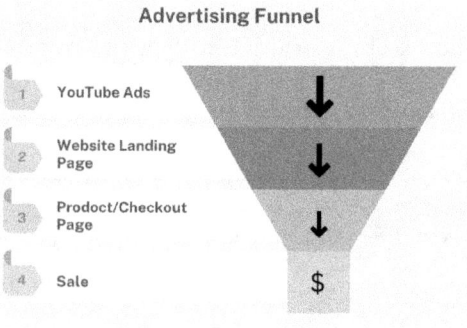

Advertising Funnel

1. YouTube Ads
2. Website Landing Page
3. Prodoct/Checkout Page
4. Sale

Creating great paid advertising funnels isn't just about the ads. Instead, each step of the funnel must be optimized to get as many people as possible to the next stage. In the theoretical case, let's say that 1 million people see the YouTube ad of a small business. Out of the 1 million, just 10,000 click on the ad and progress to the landing page. Then, just 1,000 progress to the product checkout page, and 100 convert into a sale. At any stage, a bad step in the funnel (say, a bad website, ad, or checkout page) could drastically impact results. In this manner, each stage must be worked on to ensure that the best possible overall funnel is created. Let's explore tips to create and improve each step of the funnel.

At the top of a paid advertising funnel is an ad, which gets shown to users of a given medium, such as a social networking website. Ads usually are the lowest-converting stage of the entire funnel since users are over-exposed to ads on most platforms. While the subject of ad creation will be explored thoroughly throughout the per-ad platform sections, focus on these key things across the board (and across all platforms) when creating ads:

Create with your audience in mind. You aren't creating an advertisement for everyone. You're creating ads designed to resonate with your audience (your future customers). Keep that group and their specific problems in acute focus.

Copywriting/speaking. Depending on the format (photo, video, text, etc.), you have a brief time in which to communicate a message to your viewers. In video ads, you must have a concise hook (depending upon length), while in photo and text-based ads, a catchy headline is imperative. Work on simplicity and incorporate the brand taglines identified in the brand strategy section. Ensure, above all, that if you were in the shoes of a potential customer, you would keep watching your own ad (ask some friends too—you may be a little biased).

Design (visuals). Visuals, or images, are dependent upon the type of advertisement you choose to produce. Video ads are visually different from graphics, or from text ads. When it comes to video ads, visuals and design elements should support and further the messaging and call-to-action. Think back to the brand strategy section and base design on those choices. Consider pacing and length—you want to produce just a 15-second video ad, or perhaps a longer 2-minute video. These choices will be considered in-depth throughout the YouTube ads section. For photo-based ads, it is even more critical that visual elements support the messaging and call-to-action of the ad. Keep it simple and on-brand.

Message. Beyond the initial hook, great product-focused advertisements clearly impart the value of their business and offering to viewers. Most identify or allude to a problem and describe the solution being offered, often in a manner that incorporates social proof. No matter the type of advertisements you produce, keep the messaging in mind, and keep it short and powerful.

Call-to-Action. Call-to-actions encourage customers to take the actions leading to your KPI. Call-to-actions may take the form of "buy now", "book a call", or "learn more." Whatever it is, ensure it's visually clear and direct. Consider offering some sort of incentive beyond the value proposition of the business, such as a discount, trial, or reward, and aim to increase urgency.

Following conversions derived from ads, customers are usually directed to a landing page of some sort. A landing page is a standalone web age created specifically for a marketing campaign. Alternatively, you can direct viewers to a social profile of your business on which you're looking to grow a following. The landing page typically funnels users to the final stage of the funnel, whether that's joining an email list, visiting the geographic location of a store, or buying a product online. When creating landing pages or websites, consider these best practices:

Clearly communicate a message. Most people will click off your landing page near-immediately. Your page must have a strong headline that concisely imparts the value of the page (why a viewer should stick around). You can use the tagline of your business or offer a discount. No matter how you do it, make sure someone in your target audience who has no prior exposure to your business will want to stick around.

Vibrant visuals and compelling copy. This ties into your brand strategy as a whole—ensure that the visuals (which are a must!) and the colors of the landing page communicate the vibe of the business. For example, if you're a personalized interior design agency, you may opt to go for light, friendly colors and images of happy clients and team members. If you offer operations consulting to corporate customers, you may utilize a darker and more refined color set with data-driven visuals. Additionally, ensure your headline is followed up by concise but powerful copywriting. Testimonials, photos with customers, and social proof visuals (anything that communicates you're real and professional) all work well.

Strong call-to-action. Your call-to-action drives viewers of the page to perform an action that pushes them further along your funnel. For example, "download", "get it now", and "book a call" are all call-to-actions. Ensure that the call-to-action on your landing page is clear and that all elements on the page lead viewers to it. You may offer some sort of discount or reward to encourage people to take the call to action.

Ensure that the call-to-action signup process is not difficult. Clicking on "book a call" and then having to fill out pages of personal information, for example, is sure to drastically reduce sign-up rates even once the call-to-action button is clicked. Rather, simplify and shorten the customer experience as much as is reasonably possible.

We've now explored the big-picture steps involved in creating a paid advertising funnel—first the ad, then the landing page, and finally the call-to-action and resulting behavior. We'll now progress into a description of the top ad platforms and the gritty best practices for each.

Google Ads

Google Ads is the quintessential search engine ad platform. It serves ads to the 70,000 people Googling something every second and to its four-odd billion users overall.

Google Ads average a click-through rate of 2%, meaning that one user in fifty clicks on a regular ad. 1.2 million businesses use Google Ads, while businesses make on average $2 in revenue per each ad dollar they spend.

In sum, Google Ads is a powerful tool for all types of businesses. The platform is built upon a PPC, or pay-per-click, model. This means that you only pay when your ad is clicked on—if 1 out of 100 people click on the ad, you only pay for the one click, not the hundred views (known as impressions). Keep the following terms in mind not only when it comes to Google Ads, but all PPC ad platforms:

- A **keyword** is a word or phrase searched by users who see your ad.
- Click-through rate, known as **CTR** or **CTW**, is clicks divided by impressions, or the number of people who clicked on your ad versus the number of people who saw it (e.g., if one in one hundred people click on an ad, the CTR is 1%).
- A **bid** is how much you're willing to pay for each click. Ad platforms work like auction houses: given that many businesses are competing for the same keywords, only the ad with the highest bid gets the placement.[1]

---

[1] This is a simplification. Stick with it for now, but keep in mind that quality counts, not just bid price.

- Your **CPC**, or cost per click, is the cost of ads divided by the number of clicks.
- **ROAS**, or return on ad spend, is equivalent to total conversion value (e.g., units sold, or customers generated) divided by total costs. It is similar in this manner to ROI, though keep in mind that it is based upon revenue divided by costs, not profit.

With these terms in mind, visit **ads.google.com** to get started with Google Ads. Note that Google gives $500 in free ad credit to first-time users who spend $500 on ads.

Once you sign up with your business email, follow a few brief setup steps. You'll arrive at the "now it's time to write your ad" page.

When writing copy, focus on keeping it simple. You have limited space, so think back to your target audience and message. Include a call to action, and make sure your ads line up with what viewers will experience when they click on the ad and progress down the funnel. Use social proof, and if you intend to advertise locally, make clear that you service a specific local area.

On the next page, choose specific and relevant keywords that you imagine someone interested in your product or service would search. Then, specify the locations in which you want your ad to show. If you're a business with a physical location, go hyper-local. If not, choose areas that most represent the demographic you're aiming at.

Finally, choose a reasonable budget (start small, but not small enough that results will be difficult to measure). Once you add payment info, you're ready to go! Just confirm that the $500 credit offer is applied to your account (viewable as you add payment information).

The Google Ads algorithm incorporates a quality score into bids. For this reason, new accounts and campaigns may take some time to get up and rolling—understand that this is Google figuring out the quality of your ad, not any fault of yours.

As you continue using Google ads, consider the following strategies and best practices:

- **A/B test headlines and descriptions.** The advertising game is all about testing as many ads and keywords as is reasonably possible, and sorting through them to identify the best performers. To do this, perform A/B tests by creating new ads that change just one variable of top-performing ads. For example, if targeting people in Canada with the search term "buy camera gear" is your top-performing ad, try advertising with that same keyword in the United Kingdom. Split testing in this manner over time, as well as layering on demographic and interest areas (on other platforms as well as Google), is the tried-and-true formula for long-term PPC success.

- **Eliminate low-performing keywords and locations over time.** By testing out lots of keywords and consistently removing the lowest-yielding ones, you'll build up to the most profitable, least-cost ads.

- **Advertise on competitors' keywords.** If people search for competitors that offer similar products or services to yours, they'll likely be interested in your products and services as well. So, simply add the names of your competitors as keywords that your ads will display on. When using this strategy, focus on what differentiates you from the competition in the headlines and descriptions.

Note how these strategies play out in a book promotion I'm currently running (below). The ad is operating at a low 1% CTR and a similarly low $0.05 CPC. Given that approximately 3% of clicks convert to a sale and the average profit derived from each sale is $3.5, the ad is generating a profit ROAS of 1.8, or

$1.8 in gross profit per every dollar spent on advertising.

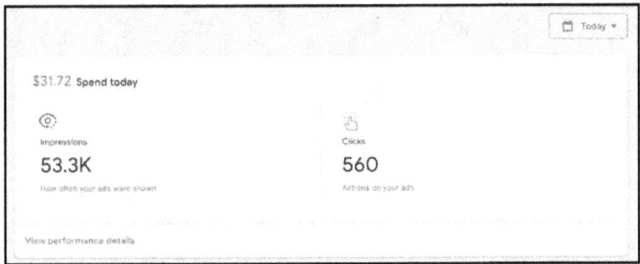

In addition to these overarching strategies, here are some tools that can help you to identify keywords and optimize ads:

- **SEMrush**: powerful keyword research and analysis.
- **SpyFu:** keyword tracking and competitor research.

- **Answer the Public**: see what people are searching.
- **ClickCease**: prevent click fraud and click farms.
- **Dashword**: optimize ad copy.

I'll conclude by restating that Google is the single-largest ad platform in the world by far, with billions of consumers clicking on its ads. Give it time and understand that profitability isn't just dependent upon luck when it comes to PPC success, but rather the work you put in to optimizing campaigns.

YouTube Ads

As the world's leading video-sharing site, YouTube logs over two billion unique visitors per month. Relative to text-based Google ads, YouTube lets you get in front of an audience in a highly visual—and if done right, engaging—manner.

Since Google owns YouTube, YouTube Ads can be setup on the Google Ads platform, and YouTube lets you advertise videos in Google search results.[2] We'll focus on video advertising within the YouTube platform.

---

[2] As well as advertise text-only ads within YouTube.

YouTube Ads can be used to increase engagement and increase subscriber growth on a YouTube channel, or (as is more popular) to drive viewers down a funnel to ultimately engage with a given business. In the below campaign of mine, note the dirt-cheap CPV, or cost-per-view. Essentially, for about $100, this campaign was able to effectively 10x the average view count of the channel at the time, display the ad to nearly 300,000 people in the vicinity of the business behind the channel, and generate significant subscriber traction.

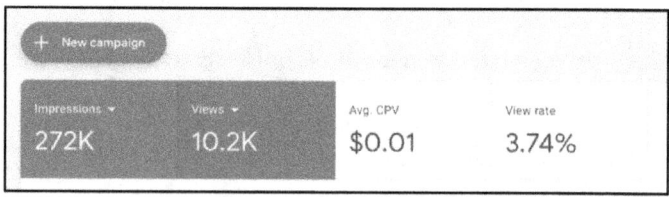

Alternatively, note the below campaign, which was designed to generate clicks and drive customers to a website. Either of these contrasting models, or some combination of the two, can be used as per your digital and social strategy objectives.

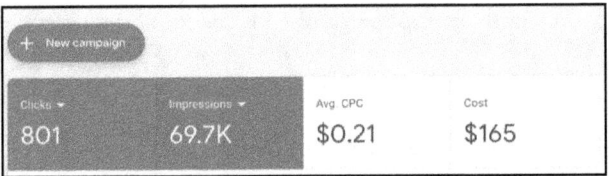

Now, note the different kinds of YouTube ads, as follows:

Skippable in-stream video ads: these ads play before (pre-roll) or during a video (mid-roll) and can be skipped after five seconds. As in the PPC model, you only pay if a viewer clicks on the ad or watches either the whole video (if sub-thirty seconds in length) or the first thirty seconds.

Non-skippable in-stream video ads: since most YouTube viewers automatically skip ads at the five-second mark, YouTube offers non-skippable in-stream ads. These ads, which can be up to 15 seconds in length, cannot be skipped by users, and play either before or during a video. However, YouTube charges for impressions for non-skippable ads, as opposed to per-click or per-view. So, the increased cost of non-skippable ads must be weighed against the increased engagement.

Discovery ads: these ads show up alongside search results as opposed to before or during a video. As opposed to viewers directly watching the video, they have the option of clicking on it and being directed toward the associated video or channel. Discovery ads allow for three lines of text in addition to a video, and for this reason, are good for businesses with snappy copy (especially copy scripts that worked well on other ad platforms) and a lesser focus on the video-only approach.

To set up an initial campaign, sign into your Google Ads account or sign up at ads.google.com (note that the $500 credit on your Google ads account can also apply to YouTube Ads).

Click "new campaign." Choose a campaign objective, just as you would when setting up a Google ad, and when selecting campaign type, make sure to choose "video." [3] You may need to set up conversion tracking, which is a simple website integration, depending on the objective you choose.

---

[3] You may also directly reach the video ad setup page by Googling "youtube ads."

Then, select the campaign subtype (one of the ad types described above). Ignore "outstream" and "ad sequence" for now. Choose the language of the ad, the locations where you want to advertise, the campaign goal (going with the automatic selection is fine, and no need to set a target cost per action as a first-time user), and your budget.

You can now create a custom audience, which incorporates demographics, interest, and remarketing (e.g., users who have already engaged with your content or website). Design your custom audience around the target audience you defined for your business in the brand strategy section. Make sure not to be overly specific, or else the reach of the ad will be limited. As for placements—if you're new to online advertising, cast a wide net through a few dozen keywords, topics, and placements that fit your target audience. Google will do this for you based on the content of the video you advertise with, so you can also opt to leave placements as "any."

You may need to add content for a companion banner—if so, just let Google autogenerate it for you. Finally, make sure to choose a strong call-to-action and headline for display under the video advertisement.

You're now ready to click "create campaign." Your ad should start running within a few hours. Keep these strategies and tips in mind as you continue to operate YouTube Ads:

Ensure your **Google Ads account is linked to your YouTube channel**. To do so, click "tools and settings", "setup", and "linked accounts."

Set YouTube ads to unlisted. YouTube ads must be uploaded to YouTube. If you intend to use videos for ads but don't want them public on your main channel, just set the visibility to "unlisted" in the video settings. Additionally, download the YouTube studio and Google Ads apps for on-the-go analytics.

In a study by Unskippable Labs, **30-second skippable YouTube ads were found to have the highest view-through rate (VTR).** The first five or so seconds are the most important—focus an ad on the value proposition, pitch, tagline, or offer made in that initial timespan.

Design ads specifically for mobile or desktop viewing. Ads for mobile viewing should have large and clear text and graphical elements. Desktop allots more space for creative elements and design features.

Leverage campaign experiments. Campaign experiments (similar to A/B testing on Facebook, as is coming up) let users copy ads and change one or multiple variables. This lets you test how changing certain variables, such as keywords, landing pages, or audiences, affects ad performance.

Quality wins. So does authenticity. Quality and authenticity represent two contrasting approaches to advertisements—say, a Superbowl-feel advertisement with famous actors, complex sets, and visual effects versus a person recording on their iPhone 6 in their living room. Both themes work—take some time to think about what kind of overarching ad theme and style fits your brand and communicates with your audience in the best manner possible. Bringing in outside help to create great ads is nearly always the right move.

Learn from competitors, and from yourself. If competitors offering similar products or services to yours have been running YouTube ads for some time, they probably have something figured out. Use their ads as a data point when considering how to design your ads and campaigns. Additionally, if you've found success on other ad platforms, incorporate those learnings into your YouTube ad creation and optimization process. Your summed marketing activities (especially among digital ad platforms) are best viewed as a network that exponentially learns what works and what doesn't over time.

We've now covered YouTube ads—next up is the behemoth of social ads.

Facebook Ads

While Google may be the quintessential search engine (browser) ad platform, Facebook is the classic social media ad platform. Facebook has nearly three billion monthly active users, while the average conversion rate (CTR) of Facebook ads is right around 9%, and 41% of surveyed retailers said their ROAS was highest on Facebook. Facebook is also a powerful ad platform in that it provides a range of tools to let advertisers accurately target the people it seeks to reach, such as through interests, behaviors, history, and so on. While the targetability of Facebook ads has decreased in recent times because of privacy concerns, it still presents very powerful targeting tools relative to most major ad platform.

Facebook ads are integrated with Instagram (since Meta, formerly Facebook, owns both Facebook and Instagram) to the extent that ads created through Facebook can be run simultaneously on Instagram.

Finally, Facebook has a "Meta pixel" (formerly Facebook pixel) which is a piece of code added to your website. This lets you effectively track the actions that customers take through Facebook ads to better monitor conversions and bottom-line metrics. The Facebook pixel also lets you retarget customers later, as it tracks their actions once they visit your website and aggregates that data to automatically optimize ads. Pixels can even be set up on your website even before you start using Facebook ads.

To do so, go to "events manager" under "all tools" at business.facebook.com. Click "connect data sources", "web", and then select "Meta Pixel." Click connect, then give it a name and enter your website URL. You'll be able to automatically connect to WordPress. If you opted to use any other website provider than WordPress, search for a tutorial on how to manually install the pixel into that system.

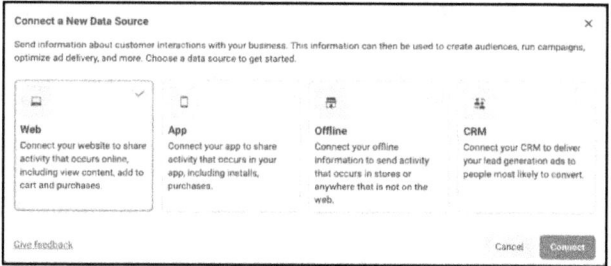

Once the pixel is integrated, you can set up events. Events are actions that people take on your website, like purchasing a product, joining an email list, or booking a meeting. While you can set up events manually, it's easiest to do so through the event setup tool, which can be found in the Meta Events Manager.

With the pixel properly installed and events created, let's explore the Facebook ad platform and campaign setup.

Confirm you're logged into your Facebook business account. Then, visit facebook.com/adsmanager/manage/campaigns, which brings you straight to the ads manager. Make sure to download the Meta Ads Manager app for mobile analytics.

Next, click the "create" button under campaigns and choose a campaign objective. Most small businesses opt for sales, leads, or awareness. Once chosen, you'll be redirected to the new campaign page. Facebook ads operate on the following three levels:

Campaigns define the top-level goals of your advertising, such as the objective, and make it easy to group different campaigns by their assigned purpose.

Ad sets are one level below campaigns and define a certain audience that advertisements are shown to. Here, you'll also set budget, schedule, and bids. Finally, an **ad** is what customers see. At the ad level, you'll add text, visuals, and a call-to-action button.

Campaigns	Ad sets	Ads

So, each ad set can have multiple ads, and each campaign can have multiple ad sets. During setup, you'll be prompted to create one campaign, one adset, and one ad.

Back at the campaign setup screen, choose a name, keep "A/B test" off (as it's easiest to do this in the ads manager toolbar), turn on "advantage campaign budget" and press next.

Now, on the ad set creation page, you can define the audience you want to reach. Connect your pixel, turn on "dynamic creative", and set a budget. It's best to split your budget across many ads (to ultimately funnel down to the top-performing ads) as opposed to spending it all on one single ad.

Next, choose your audience. Audiences can be customized based on location, age, gender, connections, demographics, interests, languages, and behaviors. Again, ads are really about experimentation, so you should aim to test a variety of audiences over time. For now, customize the audience to the normal type of customer you serve. Don't feel the need to use all the targeting options—if your customer base isn't biased toward a certain gender, for example, simply leave it as "all genders." While it's usually better to keep the audience selection specific to begin with, make sure your chosen audience isn't too small. If not, you won't be able to generate enough impressions nor meaningful conversions. Keep "advantage detailed targeting" on and make sure to save the audience for further use and A/B testing. Leave "cost per result goal" blank for now.[4]

You can now progress to the ad setup page. Ensure the connected Facebook and Instagram accounts are correct. Then, choose the format, and note that "carousel" is best to display multiple images or videos detailing your offerings or business.

---

[4] As cost per result varies widely, so it's best to only set a goal after you've established a baseline.

Custom media PPC ads are best—as with YouTube ads, people notice quality graphics, photos, and videos. More importantly, nearly everyone will immediately scroll past bad ones. Focus on simplicity and attractive visuals. As always, make sure to incorporate elements of your brand strategy.

When designing your ad and writing copy, think about the value proposition of the ad—you need something so sticky or enticing that people are sure to investigate. This could be a big discount, a unique product, a local service, or a heart-wrenching message. Whatever it is, make sure it's made clear in the headline, primary text, and graphics. Ad specs are as follows:

- **Image ads**: Size: 1,200x628 pixels. Ratio: 1.91:1.

- **Video ads**: File size: 2.3 GB max. Thumbnail size: 1,200 x 675 pixels.
- **Carousel ads**: Image size: 1,080 x 1,080 pixels.
- **Slideshow ads**: Size: 1,289 x 720 pixels. Ratio: 2:3, 16:9, or 1:1.

Make sure to fill out the five possible options for headline and description text (again, work backward to identify top performers from a strong starting set). Don't go keyword heavy or attempt to sound overly clickbaity—just communicate your value.

Finally, choose a relevant call-to-action button. Once done, you've successfully built a campaign, ad set, and ad. All that's left is to click publish.

Follow the same strategy outlined in the Google Ads section of splitting your budget across several ads and adsets, removing bottom performers, A/B testing top performers, and continuing this process over time (or to the extent that best serves your business). To end off, here are some quick tips to consider:

- Create Facebook Canvas ads—while higher-effort to create, they're proven to increase engagement.
- Increase post visibility through the "engagement" objective.
- Leverage the "lookalike audience" tool.
- Choose to only place ads on desktop or mobile (whichever fits your funnel better).

This concludes Facebook ads. Note that privacy changes are forcing Facebook to update its tracking mechanisms often. This book will be updated every year to reflect current conditions as accurately as possible but understand that the setup process may differ over time.

Instagram Ads

Facebook Ads automatically display on Instagram. This section concerns the "promoted posts" feature on Instagram, which lets users promote Instagram posts as if they were ads. Instagram ads are a great way to increase exposure and rapidly gain a following on Instagram.

To promote posts, sign into a business (professional) Instagram account. Navigate to "ad tools" and tap "choose a post." Choose the post you want to promote—if you haven't yet hooked up your Instagram account to the Facebook page of your business, now's the time.

Then, set the goal of the ad, customize the audience you want to reach, and choose your budget. Your ad will start running shortly—stay up to date with analytics either through the analytics button on each post or the "ad tools" button.

If you have an Instagram shop attached to your page, you can tag your products in a post, and then boost that post to include them in an ad.

While Instagram ads are not as likely to deliver asymmetric results compared to platforms such as Google or Facebook, they are notably stable and consistent in the results they deliver, and as stated, a great way to increase exposure and grow a following.

Consider the analytics from a small-scale post promotion of mine. $200 in ad spend generated about 1,400 likes, 70 shares, and 5,881 profile visits, which converted to several hundred new followers. On a relatively small account, this was a great boost to the growth of the page and the exposure of the post.

Unfortunately, Instagram does not currently offer rewards to first-time Instagram Ad users. If you would like a credit to create an ad through Facebook that could be shared on Instagram (without the engagement and exposure benefit of promoting a post), refer to the Facebook ads section.

We've now covered the main ad platforms: Facebook, Instagram, Google, and YouTube. We'll now explore a second tier of ad platforms: Nextdoor, TikTok, Pinterest, Snapchat, and Amazon.

Nextdoor Ads

This section was written with insight from Blake Martin, who used Nextdoor Ads to grow his curb painting business to six-figure profit as a high schooler. Nextdoor is a powerful networking and lead-generation tool for businesses serving a local clientele.

Featuring 70 million users, Nextdoor leverages community to help businesses grow—in fact, 88% of people shop at a local business at least once per week and 44% say they are willing to spend more at local businesses. So, leveraging Nextdoor as a megaphone to reach your local community through advertising and organic content is an absolute imperative for businesses with physical locations or serving a local community.

We'll examine several outreach techniques that are proven to have a beneficial effect on many small businesses. All businesses should set up their business page and share an initial post introducing their business on the Nextdoor platform; if your business offers low-ticket items and benefits most from a recurring local client base, regularly posting organic content is a prime strategy (relative to advertising, which we'll explore further on).

Within the initial post, follow either the *sell yourself* format or the *sell your client* method. The *sell yourself* method is classic, but effective all the same. Start by introducing your business to the community in a personable manner (incorporate your story as much as possible) and then state what differentiates you as a business relative to others within your community (include relevant visuals). As a first-line example: "Hello, my name is Daegan. I'm a hairstylist in San Francisco specializing in solving hair loss."

Nextdoor has an older audience than the typical social media app, so Daegan stood out by providing a solution to a problem commonly found among older demographics. Replicating this within your Nextdoor pitch is dependent upon where you live—just analyze the age groups and demographics in your community.

Within the post, also include the pricing for your product/service and close with contact info and store location (if relevant), as well as discounts or rewards. You can think of this initial

The second post format, called the *sell your client* method, is all about getting your customer to consider the benefits they would experience from your products or services. For example, as opposed to Daegan simply describing his business, he could post a before and after photo of his hair loss treatment. By describing a regular customer and how he solves their problems, people who fit the target customer profile will react strongly—in essence, get the viewer thinking about what your product/service could do for them through visual cues, testimonials, and enticing language.

Most importantly, make sure your posts tell a story. On Nextdoor, you don't want to sound like a generic advertisement, but at the same time, don't make your business sound like a hobby. Rather, tell a relatable, professional, and engaging story that ends with a call to action. Make sure to engage once you share the post—responding to comments goes a long way to strengthen connections.

In sum, you'd be surprised at the impact one strong Nextdoor post can have on your business. Apps like Nextdoor tend to exemplify the snowball effect—if your post blows up, everyone within a community will feel obliged to give your business a go, driven by FOMO and a desire to support local entrepreneurs.

Beyond organic content, advertising via Nextdoor is a powerful tool ideal for businesses selling high-ticket items or services. Note that Nextdoor ads do not run on a PPC model—instead, you pay upfront, and ads mix with organic content on the Nextdoor "home" tab. Since Nextdoor shows users relatively few ads relative to most other social platforms, conversions are usually better even if tracking and analytics are worse.

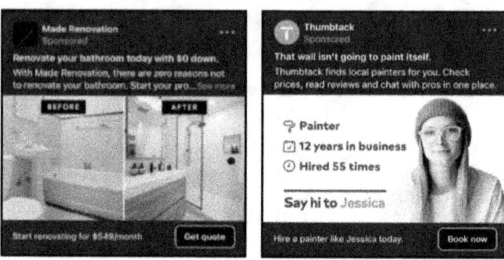

To get started, visit business.nextdoor.com. Click "claim your free business page" and make sure you're signed in with your personal Nextdoor account. Enter the name, address, and categories (choose multiple!) of the business. Upon clicking "create page" you will be directed to an ad creation page. Choose a goal for your campaign: "get more direct messages" is best for businesses selling high-ticket items or those built on lead gen, "increase website visits" is best for a business selling a range of products online, and "promote a sale or discount" is best, as may be guessed, when you have a strong sale or incentive to promote. Depending on the campaign goal you choose, complete the following step through one of two options:

Get more direct messages. Write some custom prompts detailing FAQs and questions potential customers are likely to ask. Fill out no less than three and no more than seven.

Promote a sale or discount & increase website visits. For ad content, focus on relatability and uniqueness. Identify top selling points and taglines from the brand identity section (for the headline), and use surveys, statistics, and testimonials as social proof (for the image). Ensure the click-through link goes to an optimized landing page and the call-to-action button fits with the landing page.

Then, consider the area you're looking to market your ads throughout. To do this, analyze where your current customers live, how they find you, and how far they'd be willing to drive for your product or service. Starting-uber local and expanding over time is usually the way to go.

Finally, set the budget, and click publish. Since Nextdoor ads are not based on a PPC model, upgrading and optimizing ad campaigns over time is largely a matter of running many, low-cost adverts ($3-$10 per day) and transitioning ad spend over time toward top performers.

Nextdoor really has done wonders for my business, and I'm a firm believer it can do the same for many businesses that rely on their local community to grow and thrive. Maybe your neighbor will be your best customer after all!

TikTok Ads

TikTok has recently taken the ad world by storm, and many online sellers are speaking of it as a gold rush. TikTok ads work best for businesses looking to target audiences under 30 years old with products or services that are offered online (e.g., don't try to advertise locally on TikTok). TikTok ads distribute across other apps in the TikTok network, notably Pangle and BuzzVideo.

All TikTok ads are short-form and vertically oriented; extremely short works best, so under the 15-second mark (though even shorter is often better). Visually appealing, as well as punchy messaging, is a must.

When setting up your first campaign, you'll be prompted under "create new" to choose the ad placements: you can either opt for auto-placement, where TikTok chooses for you, or go manual and select where you want your ads to show. It's initially best to either go with auto-placement or to test a wide variety of manual placements on a constrained budget. You can then build out custom audiences much as you would on Facebook (note that TikTok "ad groups" are equivalent to Facebook "ad sets"). Note that TikTok has a pixel similar to that of the Facebook pixel.

As a final note, I wouldn't recommend pushing TikTok videos as ads simply to increase exposure and grow a following. TikTok is just not difficult to grow on through organic content relative to nearly every other social platform and reaching anywhere near break-even through ads designed to increase exposure is implausible. I worked with one company that had been putting thousands of dollars into TikTok ads for that exact purpose—their account, despite being verified and having a large social team, ran itself into the ground and accumulated only a few hundred thousand likes, which translated into a sub-10k following and a near-complete loss in terms of ROAS.

Instead, leverage in-feed TikTok ads to encourage users to visit a landing page. Get going at getstarted.TikTok.com.

Endnote

There you go! That's your quick-start introduction to the six dominant pay per click advertising platforms. We haven't covered everything, but we have covered the basics that give you the ability to immediately start using thse platforms successfully, and to use this text as a springboard for further learning.

With that said, best of luck in using paid advertising to grow your business. We're cheering you on!

© 2024

ⁱ Nextdoor: Made Renovation, Thumbtack

www.ingramcontent.com/pod-product-compliance
Lightning Source LLC
LaVergne TN
LVHW021304080526
838199LV00090B/6017